Camping
For Mere Mortals
... it ain't no five star hotel.

by Michael Hodgson

Illustrations by
John McMullen

ICS Books, Inc.
Merrillville, Indiana

Camping for Mere Mortals

Printed in U.S.A.

 All ICS titles are printed on 50% recycled paper from pre-consumer waste. All sheets are processed without using acid.

Dedication

The book is dedicated to my wife Karen who, despite my eager attempts at experiencing outdoor adventures, always manages to see us safely back home.

Published by:
ICS Books, Inc.
One Tower Plaza
107 E. 89th Avenue
Merrillville, IN 46410
800-541-7323

Library of Congress Cataloging-in-Publication Data

Hodgson, Michael.
    Camping for mere mortals : -- it ain't no five star hotel / by Michael Hodgson ; illustrations by John McMullen.
        p.   cm.
    Includes index.
    ISBN 0-934802-35-1 : $6.99
    1. Camping.   I. Title.
GV191.7.H53   1992   92-21968
796.54--dc20   CIP

Table
of
Contents

Other Books by the Author

Mountain Biking for Mere Mortals

The Basic Essentials of
Minimizing Impact on the Wilderness

The Basic Essentials of
Weather Forecasting

Foreword
by Patrick McManus

When my friend Michael Hodgson asked me to write a foreword to his new book, *Camping for Mere Mortals*, I was hesitant to do so. I have long enjoyed the reputation of being the world's most miserably incompetent outdoorsman, and there was no little risk that Michael might capture that honor for himself. He is at present lost in the mountains, however, so I have decided to take a chance on the foreword.

Michael has personally field-tested every possible mishap and embarrassment ever to occur to a mere mortal on a camping trip. Indeed, he is frequently the cause of the embarrassment or mishap. He understands well the basic purpose of camping, which is to go out into the wilds and endure hardship and then come home and brag about one's own fortitude in the face of extreme adversity, such as the lack of room service. He is the guy who insists that leaves are an adequate substitute for toilet paper (and the guy who walks funny). He burns the pancakes and calls them "Cajun Flapjacks." His camping ingenuity knows no limit. If a flamethrower is needed, he can turn a simple camp stove into one with the flick of a match. On a moment's notice, "Hairless Hodgson," as he is known in camping circles, can fashion a surface-to-air missile or a tent-seeking rocket out of nothing more than a gas lantern and a cigarette lighter, always great crowd-pleasers. Anyone seeking misery on a camping trip will come home fully satisfied after an outing with Michael Hodgson. On the other hand, those interested in do-it-yourself camping misery may wish to start with Michael's *Camping for Mere Mortals*.

Camping for Mere Mortals offers some wonderful camping tips. For example, Michael heard somewhere that mosquitoes tend to avoid biting persons with lower-than-normal body temperature. He tested this by immersing himself in a freezing mountain lake long enough to lower his body temperature to the minimum required for sustaining life. Then he offered his naked body up to a cloud of ravenous mosquitoes and received not a single bite, although it is unclear from his account whether the mosquitoes avoided him because of his body temperature, froze to death on his skin before they could draw blood, or were simply repelled by his nakedness. As far as I can determine, the reason Michael conducted this scientific experiment in the first place was that he forgot his mosquito repellent. It was probably at home on the kitchen table, next to the toilet paper.

Among Michael's numerous other theories is one to the effect that invigorating mountain air produces uncontrollable lust in campers (which is another good reason to avoid camping with him). His section on sex and the camper deals at length on such matters as pine needles, pine cones, sharp rocks, mosquitoes, and poison ivy, until immersing one's self in an icy lake to lower body temperature seems a preferable alternative.

As Michael explains, the typical camping trip is wonderfully enhanced by getting lost. For sheer entertainment, he finds nothing matches getting lost, followed immediately thereafter by the cleansing effect of a spontaneous solo or group panic. Getting lost provides enormous enrichment and hilarity to the tales told about the camping trip at a later date—if there is a later date.

Michael is one of the leading authorities on getting lost. I spent a day hiking with him not long ago and was tremendously impressed. Our hiking party spent the night in a hotel in Bakersfield, California and got up before dawn to hike through Sequoia National Forest. Twice we had to send out search parties to look for him. Several members of the group started to worry about him, but I said, "Look, Michael can take care of himself. He's got plenty of food and water and a compass. He's an expert at getting lost. And one thing we know for sure, he's still here in the hotel someplace."

Camping for Mere Mortals captures the true essence of camping, and makes you wonder why you ever left home before you even leave home. But it also makes you want to get out there and taste some of that fine and pleasant misery for yourself. Imagine, if you will, yourself camped out on a high-mountain lake, listening to the hungry drone of mosquitoes and the air softly hissing from your airmattress. The sky is crystal clear and a twinkle with an infinity of stars, the embers of your campfire are dying out one by one, and from somewhere off in the darkened forest comes a long, mournful cry—probably just Michael Hodgson, still looking for the trail.

Preface

If you are a mere mortal and of the male persuasion you never, I repeat, never want to get lost in the woods with a woman. Especially one who holds a title of supreme authority, such as Wife. Come to think of it, the reverse is also true; if you're a woman you probably don't ever want to get lost in the woods with a man, especially since men have a genetic inability to admit failure or request help, even during a dire emergency when getting help seems the most obvious solution.

"George, you just lie still and I'll go get help."

"No way Martha, I told you . . .I'll find my legs any minute now."

Forget everything you have read or watched on TV, there is nothing romantic about a man and a woman lost together in the woods. For one thing, getting lost is always the man's fault. While this may in fact be true, it is in poor taste for the female to point the misjudgment out every five minutes for the rest of eternity.

"John, Mary, I would like you to meet my husband...did you know he got us lost for over eight hours once and if it wasn't for me, we never would have found the car?" The only safe thing to do at this juncture is to retire to a corner of the room with the other "lost soulmates" and swap adventure stories over numerous beers

Where, I ask you, was the woman while the man was getting lost? Why, walking with him faithfully to the point of no return, at which point the gloves are off and the real drama begins. "I don't know why I listened to you in the first place," is a favorite response.

Gone is any hope of saving face, the man is now at the woman's mercy. Innocent mistake? In the mind of a woman, there is no such thing. Getting lost is the perfect opportunity to reassert control of the relationship.

Did you ever wonder why cavemen and pioneers (ancestors of today's merely mortal contingent) hunted alone or with other men and left the women at home? Some will tell you that it was because they were chauvinists and felt the women couldn't do things men could do. These people are wrong. It was because even back then, men realized that the one place where they could be men and assert some control over their lives was in the wilderness.

Men view the idea of getting lost as an opportunity for adventure, something new and exciting. Out with the guys, man in the wilderness. Besides, as men, we will never admit we were lost, only momentarily disoriented—so what if momentarily took three days. The point is, getting lost (ahem, disoriented) is part of the adventure and becomes yet another tale to share over a pitcher of beer with anyone who will listen.

Add a woman to the recipe and the adventure version of the tale denigrates to a humiliating version such as "The idiots forgot the map, got lost and wandered around for days looking for the car. Why, if I hadn't been there, they never would have gotten out."

Somewhere down the line, a part of our male gene pool must have forgotten the teachings of our forefathers (you know, the guys who invented golf and the phrase 'Fore!') because we actually have begun to encourage our wives to join us, to share in the experience regularly. If you feel this need, I beg you, seek counseling immediately.

Several years ago my wife and I went on a simple camping trip (one of many subsequent wilderness outings together although I should admit I am actually no longer allowed to lead our adventures anymore).

The second morning was spectacular, frost bejeweled on the tips of golden blades of grass dancing under the sun in a gentle breeze. We headed out along a nondescript trail. It didn't seem to matter that I had forgotten the topo map. We were in an area well marked by trails and after all, I was a professional guide and guides don't get lost—unless they are with their wives.

It wasn't long before I realized, something wasn't right. I knew the general direction we would have to travel to reach the car, and we were not heading that way at all.

"You're lost aren't you," my wife inquired with a certain amount of glee.

"No, but we are heading in the wrong direction. We need to be going that way." I could sense my wife probing for a chink in my armor. "I'll just scout for the trail." Scouting for the trail is a technique males use to get away from wives who are beginning to assert control. One of these days we may learn that at this point, any attempt at saving face will be futile.

I suppose that stumbling on a week-old deer carcass didn't help much either, sure didn't do much for my sense of smell. My wife began reeling me in for the kill.

"Are you sure you know where we are going?" she chimed with a hint of wicked sarcasm.

"Yesssss!" I hissed.

"But, we're not on a trail." she hissed louder.

"I know dear! If I knew where the trail was we would be on it!" Whoops!

"You don't know where the trail is? I knew it! I never should have listened to you. You just better get us out of here, now. Or go get search and rescue, I'll wait right here!" It was cold that morning but not nearly as cold as the frost of burgeoning anger building around my beloved. The icy stare that followed would have frozen a bull elk solid at 300 yards. In fact, there are some who believe the Ice

Age was caused by the cumulative effect of a year's worth of icy stares from cavewomen caused by cavemen being, well, being men.

To hear my wife tell it, the next six hours were pure muddy-poison-oak-mosquito-infested-hell and that if it weren't for her strong leadership around sunset, our bleached bones would still be up there. Forgotten is the fact that I eventually found the trail, that I sprained my ankle and knee trying to help her up steep slopes, that I got poison oak faithfully holding branches out of the way for her, and that I treated for Chinese that night.

It should be mentioned here that my wife didn't even suffer a scratch, not because of my protection though. She just won't put up with an inconvenience like a mosquito bite or poison oak.

Despite my adamant protestations that I was only momentarily disoriented, she has me where she wants me for life. I will always be "the one who got lost and nearly killed us both" in introductions.

By the way, if you should ever meet my wife at a party and want to find me, I'll be on the back porch with the other mere mortals talking about the glory of wilderness and wandering for days without a care—or any idea where we were.

1 A Test of Mortality

Before delving further into this book, it is important that you are able to classify yourself as either an expert who longs for the days of buckskin and whiskey or a (and we are proud of you if you are) consummate mere mortal who, despite all odds, continues to go camping because, well because you can't think of anything better to do.

Perhaps, for the benefit of unsure readers, I should define what I mean by camping. Camping is not heading out in a motorized vehicle, pulling into a paved site, rolling out the astroturf, setting up patio furniture, hanging potted plants, plugging in the electric bug zapper, flipping on the generator that powers the AC and TV and generally doing everything in your power to recreate your home environment in miniature.

To be officially recognized as a camper, you must shun the ways of comfort and intentionally head out into the wilds to sleep on hard ground, eat cold gruel, and hike long distances wearing a heavy pack for no apparent reason other than to

rediscover the wilder essence of life—an essence that becomes aromatically obvious on or around the second day without a shower.

The following "test" will help you classify your tendencies, which of course, we will immediately report to the appropriate government agency who will be in touch shortly. Take your time and choose the best answer.

1. The thought of going to the bathroom in the outdoors conjures up images of

    a. digging a 30 foot deep hole to accommodate the week's worth of by-products from the cook's food and the keg of beer.

    b. any place that has an amazing view and perfect solitude, except for the fact that it is next to a trail—something you never discover until bared to the world as a Scout troop marches happily by.

   c. an embarrassing wet stain on your shorts because you
     didn't account for wind drift and earth slope.
   d. there ain't no way, I can hold it for a week until I find a
     porcelain throne.

2. Finding the perfect campsite usually means
   a. Clearing the immediate vicinity of any deadfall, rocks,
     beer cans, boulders and trees that might interfere with a
     perfect view.
   b. Any site that has a perfect view, quiet solitude, a
     bubbling stream, quiet breezes and is "always just over
     the next rise."
   c. Any site that is remotely level and somewhat off the trail
     and right in the middle of the only known swarm of
     homing mosquitoes and herd of hungry bears.
   d. Anywhere they "leave the light on for you."

3. Camp cooking implies
   a. a roaring fire, a slab of meat, a lager of beer and a steaming plate of unidentifiable brown slop the cook claims are beans.
   b. any food that in theory tastes wonderful but since someone went and freeze dried it, all the flavor has since departed.
   c. any food preparation technique that calls for imagination and versatility — too much water, it's soup; too little water, it's goulash; burned beyond recognition, it's Cajun tonight.
   d. a meal that does not include one of the vital food groups such as caviar, escargot, truffles, vintage wine, fresh strawberries and Devonshire cream.

4. When a friend suggests camping, you immediately think of
   a. Camo, weaponry, living off the land, beer and "the guys."
   b. Long, arduous hikes over every high peak in the region carrying an ultralight pack loaded with minimal supplies necessary for survival.
   c. Your garage, because you know that unless you clean it now, there is no way your wife will ever give permission for you to head off to the great beyond for a weekend of male bonding.
   d. Your couch, remote control, fully stocked refrigerator, the upcoming Laker's game and the fact that unless the Laker girls are going on this trip there is no way you would even consider going.

5. Standing on top of a mountain peak gazing at the great expanse spreading out beneath your feet, you wonder aloud
   a. somewhere down there is a 10 point buck just waiting for a place on my wall.
   b. wow, there are at least 10 peaks over there I haven't even climbed yet, and that river is just begging to be run and

4

I'm at it I may as well bungee back down to the valley to save some time.

c. marveling at the surrounding beauty you realize that getting up was easy, but since you somehow dropped the rope getting back down may be a tad more difficult... HELP!

d. looks great now, but think what a condo and golf course adjacent to a five star resort hotel would do for land values—all with a view of this peak of course.

6. What does wilderness emergency mean to you?
    a. you have been mauled by the only known herd of grizzlies, trampled by 300 rams (that's mountain sheep, not the football team) and you are now forced to drag

       yourself through 200 miles of alligator infested swamp back to your car with your legs in your pack in the hopes that the doctor can reattach them.
    b. maybe you really won't be able to run faster than your partner as that bear is charging you.
    c. the stove you were using managed to explode magically turning your tent into a flambeau side dish and you into the night's main course, hiker sans hair. Good thing you brought plenty of Cheeze-Its, every camper's emergency staple diet.
    d. not having room service and the ice machine doesn't work

7. Be prepared, the Scout motto, means
    a. you can build a shelter out of rocks and twigs, nail a grasshopper at 30 feet with a stream of chewing tobacco, kill a moose for meat with your bare hands, break down and reassemble an automatic rifle in under 30 seconds

while blindfolded and play Dixie on a harmonica just in case company drops by the camp.

b. with nothing more than a compass, a cup, a sheet of plastic, matches and firestarter you can build a citadel of wilderness luxury.

c. that no matter how much stuff you carry and how much training you undertake, whatever happens will be the one thing you are not prepared for.

d. not running out of beer during the Super Bowl and never ever letting them see you sweat.

Now for the moment of truth. Total up your points giving yourself four points for each (a); three points for each (b); two points for each (c); and one point for each (d). Write your point total here_____. If you scored a perfect 28 things are not looking good. We suggest you take a shower, put down the gun and seek counseling—there is no more wild west. If you scored between 21 and 27, there is hope. While you may still have tendencies toward biting off the tops of beer cans and wearing camo, you are on the threshold. Study this book carefully and you will learn what it takes to be "A Mere Mortal." If you scored between 14 and 20 points you are a consummate mere mortal. You can take pride in the fact that while getting lost in camp or burning the water on a stove are impossible, you will find a way. This book will be an invaluable resource of information and experiences for you. Sorry, but if you scored less than 14 you must resign yourself to the fact that for you, sleeping anywhere but the Hyatt is roughing it—too bad, you're missing out on a wonderful world.

2 Packing Light; Leaving The Semi At Home

I'm tired of listening to old timers talk about "when they had it tough." These stories of climbing Mount Unbelievable with bare hands, a slab of bacon, and an old wool blanket bedroll need addressing. If we could have it so easy. Sure, they had hardships and nights were cold and dark (especially dark), but things aren't easier now, they are much tougher.

Permits

Back then you could go anywhere, anytime and on a moments notice. Now, you have to call ahead and make a reservation to get a permit to allow you to park at the concession so that you can stand in line to enter your name in a lottery to have a chance to win one of three hundred opportunities to go camping and fishing this year. Where would Teddy Roosevelt have been if he couldn't get a permit I ask you?

Stoves

How about cooking? In the old days you collected wood, built your fire, hung a pot, skewered some meat, and huddled

near the flames spinning tales about women, great hunts, and days gone by. Today we have stoves. We are forced to use stoves because, in the mid seventies, nine trillion people, all who worked for several major stove manufacturers, went into the wilderness and gathered up all the wood they could find, thereby creating a wood shortage.

In theory, stoves should make cooking more convenient and easier. You don't have to deal with lighting wet wood, going about gathering up half the forest to have enough fuel for the night, whittling a stick to skewer the meat with, or running laps around the fire-ring in a vain attempt to avoid the smoke. Instead, you pump and curse until your thumb begins to swell thereby indicating the stove has enough pressure to launch Skylab. Carefully rotating the stove three times while you turn counterclockwise once, you light a match and place it by the priming needle. This in turn causes a violent eruption singeing the hair off your face (eliminating the need for shaving) and announcing to the world that you have begun to cook.

Fuel

Fuel is the cruelest joke of all. Stove manufacturers design their stoves to calculate the amount of fuel you are planning to use for a particular trip (I am not making this up). If you are trying to cut it close and conserve on weight, the stove will naturally increase its consumption of fuel causing you to run out with several days left on your journey. This means that you will have to eat several days worth of cold freeze dried food which doesn't taste much different from hot except that it is somewhat crunchy and definitely cold. If you are tired of running out of fuel and plan to carry a reserve just in case, the stove will reduce its consumption causing you to needlessly carry 300 extra pounds of fuel over multiple 10,000 foot mountain passes.

Tents

Tents are seemingly a good thing. I will concede that the invention of the lightweight tent does give us a ready made shelter, something the old timers never had. Yet, sleeping under fancy fabric with bright colors and geodesic shapes takes something out of the glamour of camping. Gone are the days of building a shelter out of pine boughs, grass, and other handy materials. Instead we have the struggle of man against technology.

Picture this, the wind is whipping, the rain sheeting down, and the desperate camper is yelling instructions to his now irate wife. Tent fabric is flapping everywhere (or is that the wife?) as our brave camper attempts to neatly thread narrow aluminum poles through an intricate maze of tunnels even a mouse couldn't figure out. Before long the exhausted camper is locked in a death struggle with a living, seething, nylon and aluminum octopus that threatens to consume both him and the surrounding campsite. Finally, the beast is tamed and the shelter is up, just in time for the sun to break through and dry out the now saturated campers. Maybe technology is convenient, but pine boughs sure sound a lot easier.

Backpacks

Packs are definitely a major achievement. They keep getting stronger and lighter; they have to because we keep getting weaker and heavier. Not to mention all that extra stuff we are forced to carry—beer, matches, beer, first aid kit, beer, alkaseltzer, beer . . . Some packs are even big enough to carry shelter, a stove, dinner, survival gear, and someone to prepare the meal.

Survival Gear (the 10 essentials plus 1,000)

Old timers never had to carry survival gear. This is because they were smart enough to build a fire when cold, make a shelter when it rains, and come in before it gets dark. Today's camper finds it more difficult to make these independent decisions, thereby causing them to have to carry 920 pounds of survival gear to do the thinking for them. We have waterproof flashlights to help us find a survival kit buried in the bottom of a very dark pack so large that it could quite possibly hold the entire state of Texas. Of course, this flashlight has been lighting the inside of the pack since leaving home, thereby making it useless in a real emergency because the batteries are dead.

Being a true outdoorsman one does carry spare batteries, but since it is dark, they are at the bottom of the pack, and there is no light, you are left to grope and gripe. In the event that by some miracle you do find them, putting batteries in a flashlight in the dark is an entirely new exercise in frustration. Forget that you can barely see the little symbol etched discreetly on the flashlight describing positive and negative—you couldn't see them if they were floodlit. The only hope is to disassemble the flashlight and then be able to reassemble it without any leftover parts or without launching the battery spring several hundred yards from where you are groveling in search of the battery you just dropped—for the hundredth time.

There are waterproof/windproof matches that will light even when you are five hours and 30 inches of rain too late in trying to start a fire. These matches will light up a camp for several seconds, which would have been useful when assembling the flashlight, however, you needed the light to find the matches in the first place.

We have survival knives with built-in gadgets that will allow you to signal for help, fish while you are waiting for help to arrive, and then cook the fish so you will have something to serve once help gets there. Emergency blankets were invented to wrap yourself in after spending seven futile hours trying to thread tiny aluminum tent poles through narrow fabric tunnels in a downpour when you should have listened to your wife and the weatherman and stayed home.

Magnifying glasses are part of any real survival package. Most survivalists will tell you that this is so you can use the sun to start a fire. Hah! Try focusing the energy of a raindrop on a wet leaf and see how far you get. The real reason to carry the magnifying glass is so that you can read the print on the survival information cards that you also pack with you. These cards will tell you what you already know—that you are wet, cold, hungry, and damn glad you didn't listen to your wife because you would be home cleaning the garage if you had.

Then, of course, there is the signal mirror. This is used to flash imaginative signals at imaginative planes during a very unimaginative 36 hour downpour while you are wrapped in your emergency blanket staring at your $500.00 soggy pile of nylon and aluminum wishing you were home cleaning the garage.

Air Mattresses

Sleeping is another issue. Old timers just had to fluff up the dirt, lay out some nice soft pine boughs, spread out their bedroll and hit the hay. Today, mainly because the ground is harder due to the earth's decreased rotation causing hardening of the surface area (I am not making this up), and because we are a kinder and gentler nation, we are forced to fight with air mattresses. Air mattresses have two purposes. One is to deflate in the middle of the night leaving you to ponder how difficult it would be to hike out in the dark and spend the night sleeping in a motel. The other is to drift you blissfully out of a flooded tent and several miles downstream before deflating and leaving you to ponder the joys of wet down and the discovery that you are in a bag that lacks any inclination to float.

Sleeping Bags

Beyond the challenge of staying inflated all night, one has to deal with sleeping bags. Bedrolls were designed with comfort and airy space in mind. Some old timers will insist that there should be an emphasis on airy; no, I think it was breezy. Still, a mild Northeastern gale blowing over your toes is nothing compared to the challenge of sleeping in a bag that was designed to confine occupant movement while slipping down any given slope toward running water, fire, or the wettest corner of a tent. I once slid 14 miles back to my car because someone forgot to zip the downhill side of the tent closed.

Wilderness Fashion

I would be remiss if I overlooked the entire fashion issue. Old timers only had to deal in khaki, jeans, buckskins, or whatever looked the oldest and most durable. Now one has to decide between polypro or capilene, synchilla or wool, nylon or GoreTex, cobalt or fuchsia. Heaven forbid that your baggie shorts in cobalt, your synthetic shirt in red, and your purple pack should clash—what color was our tent dear?

Gone too are the days of simple decision making. Do I wear long pants or shorts, T-shirt or flannel, wool socks or cotton? To answer the question you simply checked the temperature and pulled on the available garb. With the advent of activity specific as well as temperature specific apparel, however, today's outdoor's person needs a virtual database with cross-referencing systems. You now must buy clothes for mountain biking, hiking, trail running, cross country skiing, canoeing, warm weather, cold weather, no weather, any weather, some weather, uphill, downhill, traversing, high humidity, nuclear fallout, acid rain, and those days when you just want to be you.

The end result of all this choice is a pack full of clothing for every possible occasion and then some. In fact, today's camper spends so much time agonizing over the "correct" garment for the day that often they never leave camp.

"Damnit John! I just can't figure . . .do you think I should wear the black mountain jacket complete with the pit zip, side zip, diagonal zip, neutron cold fusion mood coating or the fuchsia paddle/hike pullover with the no-pill plush pile and optional wind and bullet-proof overlay?"

"Geeze Jerry! I was thinking more in terms of the cobalt one-piece micromatique climb/cycle, world peace enhancing, full-zip with optional butt ventilation snap flap."

"Gosh John . . .maybe we just shouldn't hike today. Wouldn't want to be caught out in the wilds with the wrong equipment you know."

Checklists

Gone are the days of grabbing a bedroll, a rifle, a small sack of grub (called grub because whatever was in the bag tasted so bad it sure as heck couldn't be called food) and trudging off in whatever direction suited the fancy. Now, if someone manages to allow an independent and somewhat spontaneous thought to enter the cranium, such as "hey, lets go camping!" everyone in the group immediately reaches for their Daytimers to see if they can schedule an opportunity to get together to think about whether it is a good idea to go camping on such short notice (short notice meant to imply any proposed activity within the next six months that wasn't already factored into the schedule). Assuming that all members of the prospective adventure can agree upon a date to plan the planning meeting for the adventure, the next obstacle to be encountered is successfully negotiating THE CHECKLIST.

In theory, THE CHECKLIST is a good idea since we have become so civilized and urbanized that the potential for actually using common sense and independent planning to load a pack with sufficient gear to enjoy a weekend trip has become a virtual impossibility. In actual practice, however, THE CHECKLIST serves two insidious purposes: 1) to create so many choices and new product ideas that the poor camper-to-be either gives up in complete frustration or whips out the plastic running up so much debt that she is now forced to take a second job that no longer leaves enough time for the planned camping trip 2) leaves the poor camper-to-be so unsure of himself and the available choices that he packs everything resulting in a 7,249 pound load even a pack mule would look cross-eyed at.

Since no book on camping would be complete without THE CHECK LIST, I have dutifully assembled one for which I fully expect your undying gratitude.

✔ Check list (be sure to check that you are indeed working with a check list for your camping trip and not an old grocery list)

✔ Brain (no sense in reading any further if you don't have one of these)

✔ Leave an itinerary of your upcoming trip with someone you trust who will call out the troops if you don't come home (I recommend this person be someone you owe money to since you can bet they, above anyone, will be anxiously awaiting your safe return)

✔ Backpack (Experts will tell you to carefully check your pack for rips, tears and wear spots that might give out on the trail. What good is this? Anyone knows that if the pack gives out, you won't be able to carry any gear leaving your friends to carry everything. I can tell you from experience that hiking without a pack is pure bliss—as long as your friends don't find out you planned the whole thing)

✔ Tent (Always check your tent before heading out. That way, you can confirm that the culture of mold and

17

bacteria coating the inside of the tent, from the last time you packed it wet, is still alive and doing well. Checking a tent beforehand will also give you an opportunity to discover the inevitable singular sock that has since petrified into an unrecognizable, dirt encrusted ball suitable for use as a paperweight).

✔ Stove (Give your stove a pretrip test. First, add fuel, don't worry about the copious amounts of white gas you will inevitably spill all over the stove and surrounding area. Pressurize the stove by pumping furiously for, say, 30 or 40 minutes. Discover that you have left the flame control valve open and have been spraying an area the size of New York City with fuel. Chuckle to yourself. Close the valve, pump several hundred more times. Light match and observe how quickly you and the stove erupt into flames. Remember that you are not supposed to be on fire and douse the flame. Carefully now, open the fuel control valve and check to see that the stove's burner is working. If the stove and you become launched skyward during this process, it is probably because the stove has a tad too much pressure. Next time, pump only till your thumb turns a light shade of blue)

✔ Boots (Though as a teenager you were perfectly happy hiking in a pair of beat up Converse high tops, your feet, like your body have matured and now demand preferential treatment. Consequently, you must now purchase a pair of special shoes for hiking with more accessories, bells and whistles than you know what to do with—all in the name of providing foot pampering comfort. It probably won't be too long until some forward thinking company invents a hiking shoe that will actually do the hiking for you, set up camp and perform all the chores leaving nothing for you to do

but revel in the luxury)

✔ feminine funnels (This nifty invention allows a woman to stand and deliver like a man instead of baring her soul and posterior to the wind and world every time she needs to pee. In theory, the funnel gives any woman the opportunity to stand with the men, engage in sword fights and write her name in the snow with the best of them. In actual practice the device often spatters and drips down the legs, on your shoes and—hey!, come to think of it, that's just like a man.)

✔ Plastic spade (you will use this to bury human waste)
✔ Toilet paper (there are some back to nature groups
that advocate leaving the TP at home and resorting to
leaves, sticks, rocks or snow to wipe one's posterior. I
say, if God had intended us to wipe with leaves, he
wouldn't have created nettles, poison oak or holly—
yeowwww!)
✔ Fresh Food (you will use this to generate human waste)
✔ Freeze Dried Food (you will use this to generate human
gas and toxic odors that render an entire campsite
uninhabitable)
✔ Free Standing Tent (this tent comes with so many poles
that once assembled it resembles the scaffold used to
build the World Trade Center. All these poles are
necessary to provide the convenience of a free-
standing tent that requires no stakes—something you
immediately appreciate as you watch your $700 free-
standing tent tumble cross-country in a gentle breeze
like just another expensive tumbleweed.)
✔ Ziploc bags full of assorted emergency things you may
or may not need during the trip but are carrying
anyway just in case (suggested items are: patch kit
for your air mattress, repair kit, extra parts for the
repair kit, more parts to repair the repair kit in case it
breaks, stove parts, pack parts, parts parts, partial
parts, party favors . . .)
✔ Duct tape (it repairs anything from rips and tears to
breaks and loose parts. In fact, it is not unusual to
return from a trip looking as if everything you own was
originally made with duct tape. Of course, this begs
the question, why not make everything in duct tape to
begin with?)
✔ Compass (since the needle only tells where north,
south, east and west are, this gadget won't do you

much good. What you really need is a needle that always points the way home—now that would be really useful)

✔ Topographic Map (any map that has these squiggly brown lines all over it and looks somewhat like your four-year old has gotten to a perfectly good road map with her crayon.)

✔ Emergency Food (fancy terminology for Snickers bar)

✔ Sierra Cup (everyone used to carry one of these and if you want to be in with the really cool crowd, you will carry one too, hanging from your belt or some part of your pack where it is both visually and audibly (as it clangs and bangs against everything) obvious. The really neat thing about a Sierra Cup is its shape, narrow at the bottom and wide at the top. This nifty design allows the cup to spontaneously spill hot liquids into your lap almost daily. If, by some miracle you manage to balance the cup somewhere, its extra wide brim dissipates heat so efficiently that you are left drinking a disgustingly tepid soup that went from boiling to inedible in the space of time it took you to lift the cup to your lips)

✔ Swiss Army Knife (a very compact knife/status symbol that contains enough tools to perform a complete tune-up on an automobile engine which would be outstandingly useful if you were a car mechanic . . .since you're not, you carry all these extra tools because you never know when you might get the urge. Meanwhile, you can console yourself with the fact that it does have a very sharp blade, something you just discovered as you snapped it shut on your finger while searching for the scissors . . .now where is that first aid kit?)

✔ First Aid Kit (a wonderful little kit that contains everything you may need to perform open heart surgery but never has enough of the items you really use like Snoopy Bandaids and moleskin)
✔ Some sucker to carry everything because you sure as heck don't want to.

3 Getting To And Setting Up Camp Without Serious Injury

Packing the Pack

In general, the rule that you should keep heavy items low and near your center of gravity and lighter items up and away from your body is a good one. Of course, for many men, this would mean finding a pack that will keep all the weight loaded at or below the stomach—a practical impossibility.

Putting the Pack On

There are several approved techniques to putting a pack on your back. One is called "lift, grimace and whirl" (which is somewhat self explanatory) and the other "toss, hope and pray." I prefer the toss, hope and pray method myself since there is always the brief hope that during the toss the pack will somehow take wing and be waiting expectantly for you at camp when you arrive—this is where the pray part comes in. Upon the realization that all 500 lbs of pack have just ended their brief, albeit glorious flight, and come to roost on your back, you immediately begin praying for enough strength to make it back to the car and the short drive to the nearest 7-11.

Taking the Pack Off

You reach a rest area or camp and your only thought is for snacks, water and recuperation. Loosening one shoulder strap, you slide an arm out, grab the top of the pack and prepare to swing the 500 lb load to the ground in one energetic heave. With the other hand, you undo the waist belt and in one smooth motion you whirl the pack earthward like an experienced outdoorsman. Of course, since you forgot to undo the sternum strap the pack's entire

10,000 lbs is now left dangling from your neck reminding you that while your need for snacks, water and recuperation is great, your immediate need for oxygen is far greater.

Finding a Campsite

There is no such thing as a perfect campsite. Experienced campers know that no matter where you decide to set up camp, you will always have the feeling that a better site exists just over the next rise. If, by some miracle of miracles you do happen upon campsite nirvana, the bliss will be immediately replaced by the realization that the camp is guarded by a very voracious band of ants. Begin to cook and these ants show up with dinner plates and silverware. Decide to lie down for a brief respite under a cloud dappled sky and these same ants will decide to conduct an exploration into the deepest and darkest corners of camp, which inevitably means your shorts—yeowwww!

Setting Up Camp

It is at this point you will realize that whoever wrote the tent instructions had a wonderful sense of humor. "Insert the ferrule C of pole A into the B grommet by way of the intersecting pole sleeves [see insert and refer to page 300, illustration 223b] interconnected alphabetically and numbered sequentially to make this simple procedure easy. Now, carefully flex the pole and insert ferrule G3 into grommet 7.249f as shown on page 23)." It is a little known fact that most tent manufacturers have never set up a tent in their lives, and that they are not even sure if the instructions to the tent actually work, but they sounded so neat that they published them anyway.

The Campfire

There is an irony to camping that is best highlighted by fire. Why does it take several bales of dried newspaper, 300 lbs of kiln-dried kindling, 400 lbs of specially aged pine, and nearly a gallon of white gas to start even the faintest flicker of a campfire and yet a singular sunbeam glancing off a teeny piece of glass in the middle of

a dew-dampened meadow can set an entire forest ablaze in seconds? Humankind may never know the answer to this burning question.

Why do we need campfires? Although stoves have replaced fires as a more environmentally responsible way of cooking in the wilderness, hunkering down around a hissing flame to get warm or roast marshmallows doesn't do much for romance or contemplative reflection. After all, it is only while staring into dancing flames that great minds are stimulated and inspired to suddenly remember "Damn, I left the iron on at home, the garage door standing wide open and the car unlocked at the trailhead."

How do you build a campfire? Easy. First, you get a small bundle of tiny twigs piled over a wad of toilet paper (unused preferably). Next you light a match which gets blown out by a breeze that you didn't even know existed. You light another match, carefully shielding it with your cupped hand. The breeze you still can't feel shifts direction and blows the match out again. Light another match, this time protecting it with your hands so well that you start to sniff the air and wonder what's cooking. Looking down at the match, you realize your hand is on its way from rare to medium rare. YEORWGGRUMOPH #@*%@*. Place the entire book of matches on the twigs that you have now soaked with white gas. Light another match and throw it on the pile. BOOOOOM! In four milliseconds, the flame is shooting 300 feet high and you now have no eyebrows. Racing about like a whirling dervish for fear of the flame dying out you begin tossing all available material on the fire, clearing the forest of all debris within a 10 mile radius. Planes, mistaking your fire for a landing beacon begin to circle. After 10 or 12 hours, your fire should subside enough for you to come within a mile or two of it and actually enjoy its ambiance and warmth.

Sex in the Wilds
"Marge, I've wanted you for so long."
"John, take me . . .and don't be gentle."

So it is with sex in the wilds. Mountain air causes brain cells to hopelessly overload with hormonal impulses until, in one overwhelming surge, passion overcomes logic and couples actually believe it is going to be wonderful and extremely romantic to make love outdoors. In reality, nothing could be further from the truth. Let's pick up with Marge and John as their passion heats up to a full boil.

"Ohhh baby, Ohh Marge, Yeowwwww...(SLAP).Damn mosquitoes!"

"Ohh John, never mind, just kiss me and Yearrrggg...get those pine needles out of my..."

"Sorry Marge, lets move over here and @#%$%#* damn zipper's (SLAP) got my *$#@ caught in it."

"Ohh you poor baby (SLAP) let me help you...YEARGGG (SWAT)...stupid horsefly...I'll just move...owww those rocks hurt ...over here and...is that poison oak?"

Now, that's what I call romance...honey, let's go camping this weekend, OK?

Minimizing Impact

It has long been held that it is man's responsibility to minimize impact upon the wilderness. In reality, what is meant by that rash statement is that the wilderness traveler must do everything possible to minimize the wilderness's impact upon him or her.

- Avoid crowded dates and places: right! that means hike into a remote site 300 miles from the nearest trailhead only to find that everyone else has the same "environmentally responsible" idea on that very weekend. What's more, if everyone practices avoiding crowded dates then the crowded dates won't be crowded anymore and the rest of the year will be a mess.
- Repackage food to reduce containers and trash: Seems to me that if you are repackaging food, you are doubling the trash—

what happens to the original containers? I suspect that this rule was inserted by Congress at the behest of the powerful Ziploc lobbying organization.

- Carry out all that you carry in: I know from experience that my pack gains weight during a hike, which means I am packing out more than I started with. Will someone please explain this one to me?
- Set up camp 200 feet away from the nearest water source or trail: this is done to ensure that you will get the maximum amount of exercise during each camping trip.
- Don't wash directly in any water source—wash at least 100 feet away: Since most wilderness water sources are just about warm enough to prevent ice from forming, this is not usually a problem. And we wonder why pioneers always seemed so dirty in pictures—would you voluntarily put any part of your body in ice water to clean it? I think not.
- Always use campsites that have been used by others: You can tell a used campsite by its resemblance to pictures of the Oklahoma dust bowl in the early 1930's—no plant or wildlife within 500 yards and nothing but dirt for as far as the eye can see.
- Use established latrines when available: One can ascertain if a latrine has been established by the decidedly unique and acrid odor that accompanies such construction for a radius of five square miles.

4 Getting Lost Is An Art Form

Where the Hellawe?

There are many good books on map and compass skills as well as the art of navigation in the wilderness. I know this because loving friends have sent me every title in a gallant attempt to educate me. I am very pleased to announce, however, that their efforts have been in vain and that I am still a qualified expert on getting disoriented. Just ask my wife.

Getting properly disoriented is a highly developed skill. It is not easy to get lost on the fourth floor of Macy's nor is it easy to miss the freeway off-ramp to your own house every time, and yet I am proud to say that I have accomplished these difficult tasks and more. It is in the wilderness though, that I am at my all time best. I once led my wife into thickets of poison oak, through mud and snow, over several passes, and into the valley of death, the entire time casually explaining, "the car is just over the next rise dear."

Herein lies the importance of being an expert in disorientation—the ability to seem casual and sure of yourself in the face of impending doom. Never mind that I was dehydrated, we were out of food, and I was muttering under my cheerful breath "where the hellawe." Through it all I managed to maintain an air of confidence, a sense of calm that had my wife promising divorce (we weren't married at the time) and other sorts of nasty tortures that can only be thought up by the opposite sex in times of stress.

Armed with my extensive research in the art of disorientation and background in getting hopelessly turned around, I have decided to share my knowledge so that others can feel confident in remaining calm when everyone else should probably panic.

Mastering the Art of Staying Lost

Getting disoriented is a natural skill most humans are born with. The trouble is, through study and the invention of little gadgets with floating needles (editors note: these gadgets are commonly known as compasses) we spend our entire lives trying to hide this talent. Why fight it? Remember, the United States would not have been discovered had it not been for Christopher Columbus getting disoriented on his way to buy spices and exotic oils for his queen at a nearby department store. Who knows what great things you might accomplish just by getting disoriented?

The key to proper execution of complete disorientation is never admit that you don't know exactly where you are and always keep your composure and dignity. A fellow author and expert on getting lost, Patrick McManus, invented the Modified Stationary Panic, the Stationary Panic, and the Full Bore Linear Panic. Execution of these techniques are explained in detail in his book *A Fine and Pleasant Misery* should you wish to learn more. While panic is appropriate if you are alone, this advice is

34

not practical if you are a group leader and everyone is looking to you for a decision. It becomes increasingly important as the weather turns ugly (which it will) and night draws ever closer (which it does) that you keep calm so that the group looking to you for leadership puts down their weapons and stops using words like "kill, maim, mutilate . . ."

For example, you have planned a special family outing to a beautiful campsite you remember visiting when you were a teenager. Your kids, now teenagers themselves are ecstatic, so much so that they refuse to go unless they can share the moment with a few of their closest friends of the opposite sex. Your wife, barely able to contain her excitement asks if you have packed survival gear and the map. "I've been there a hundred times, don't worry," you comment casually. To which your wife replies, "Better let me carry the map."

One mile into the trip (or was it three?) you find yourself in the middle of a swamp, no dry land in sight and with the sudden realization that nothing looks even remotely familiar. Your family looks nervously at you and you smile knowingly back at them. "Come on then, just up and over the next ridge is camp," you say as you head off muttering "where the hellawe."

Eleven ridges and eleven swamps later (that have a decidedly curious resemblance to the eleven swamps and ridges before) your family is beginning to doubt your navigational skills. Your kids are no longer claiming you as their father and your wife is reminding anyone within earshot what a fool she was to marry you. This is when being an expert in disorientation becomes critical. Keeping your composure and dignity (quite challenging in the presence of angry family members plotting your slow death) you have several excellent options.

Scouting

First, suggest that everyone remain calm and take a break while you head off to a nearby high point to reconnoiter. (Always use important sounding words like reconnoiter in situations like this.) Going off to a high point will allow you a chance to get away from the angry mob, climb high above the woods, and yell "Where the hellawe!" If you are lucky you will recognize a landmark, like the parking lot where you left your car several hundred miles back. If you are really lucky you will run into someone who actually knows where they are and can tell you where you are—like a ranger.

If, during your reconnoiter you have occasion to fall, take full advantage of the situation. Break branches, crash into trees, bounce off rocks, and scream loudly. This is done so that any lions, tigers, or bears watching will decide to go off and hunt more challenging prey and so that you will appear as if you have had to struggle through hell itself to save your anxious family. Your family is anxious since you cunningly took the car keys with you guaranteeing that they would either have to wait for your return or walk home.

If scouting ahead is out of the question because you risk becoming disoriented during the reconnoiter, stumbling upon the car, but then being unable to find your family again, you must resort to option two. Option two involves actually using a map and that little gadget with a floating needle (experts commonly refer to this tool as a compass). Of course, you and I

both know that to be really proficient at getting disoriented you can never bother to learn how to use these ridiculous tools, but you carry them anyway for desperate occasions such as this.

Using the map

Spread out the map (it doesn't matter whether it is upside down or not since you can't read it anyway) and begin acting like you are using the little gadget with a floating needle. Calmly "Hmmm," and "Of Course," a lot to yourself as you knowingly stroke your chin, (no easy task when you have no idea what you are doing). Pretending that this is to be a tutorial lesson which they will all thank you for later, you proclaim, "Of course! I should have known where we were, I just didn't take into account declination and magnetic north." (Note the use of the fancy words again.) "It's not that hard really. Why don't one of you try to figure out where we are."

Since no one in your family can believe you actually know where you are, they eagerly grab at the map and the gadget to see for themselves. After much biting, scratching, name calling, and mud slinging your wife will gleefully exclaim "Here's where we are and there's the camp right over the next ridge," (which is what you have been telling them all along). Now that you have tricked them into revealing your location, it is a simple matter to convince them that they need more practice and should see if they can indeed find camp.

However, option two assumes someone in your group can actually read a map and use that little gadget (what's it called again, a compass?). If, after trying option two and finding all members of your group pointing in entirely different directions and screaming "Where the hellawe," you must take drastic measures. First, resist the urge to run blindly through the forest removing foliage and anything else that might get in the way. You are the leader and must act like you know where you are going, even if you can't find your way out of bed in the dark. Carefully and with dignity fold the map, put away the gadget, mention that you will continue the lesson later, but it's time to get to camp. Then, head resolutely off in any direction you choose.

You are now safe in the knowledge that, unlike Christopher Columbus, you know the world is round and that, eventually, your little group (all proud and prospective inductees to membership in the Hellawe Club) will either run into the car, camp, other hikers, or a new world. If it's a new world you're in luck, they may even name a national holiday after you.

38

5 Squawking Around The Campfire And Eating Cold Gruel With A Smile

Many years ago, as an easily influenced young lad in search of all things great and wonderful, I heard a saying that convinced me camping was the most wonderful activity of all. "Breakfast begins as soon as you wake up. Lunch commences once breakfast ends and the camper should only stop eating lunch when supper is served." Even today, as an older and wiser, well definitely older camper I find a wonderful wisdom and certain comfort in that statement.

Camp cooking

Nothing comes with quite so much notoriety and predilection to impending doom as having to prepare a meal for others in the out of doors. Camp cooking is tough enough without having to deal with a pack of unappreciative food critics. Especially when dealing with freeze-dried edibles. Too much water and you end up with an unidentifiable stew or soup. Too little water and all you get is petrified sludge. I suppose one could actually resort to measuring water accurately, but since when did reading instructions become part of a cook's responsibility?

"Golly Jason, this soup tastes like dishwater."

"That is dishwater Marge, the soup is the blob on your plate. Sorry, but I guess I didn't add enough water."

There are some very basic, though unwritten rules of etiquette when eating camp cooking. First, it is considered a backhanded compliment in most circles when one comments, "I can't believe how good this tastes when combined with outdoor air . . .I mean, I normally wouldn't touch this at home, but out here it really is quite delicious." Second, since most camp cooking gets done at dusk, most food eating occurs at night. This is a blessing in disguise since most often no one really wants to see what they are eating. It is, however, considered very cowardly and most unsportsmanlike to analyze your food with a flashlight prior to eating.

Food is generally served one of two ways in the wilderness, cold or charred. There is no in between. Either way, you risk hurting the cook's feelings unless you bravely comment "Gosh, how did you know I 'Gulp' liked chewing on oatmeal bricks so much."

Of course, sometimes that kind of gallantry can come back to haunt one.

"Wow, I never knew how good gnawing on a chunk of your special dutch oven baked cake could be sweetheart."

"That, my schnookums, is a rock. I accidentally dripped some batter on it while I was pouring the mix, but since you like it so much why don't you just keep sucking on it!"

Somemores

Whoever thought up the idea of mixing graham crackers, toasted marshmallows and melted Hershey's chocolate was warped. It's not that these ingredients are bad, or that the concept of eating the mess is almost as much fun as wearing it. The problem with this age-old dessert lies in the toasting of the marshmallow.

Mild-mannered and veteran campers, who will argue about nothing else, have been known to come to blows over the correct method and manner in which marshmallows are to be toasted. Golden brown or charcoal crisp? Delicately and properly roasted 10

40

inches from glowing coals or dipped into the fire and removed a burning mass of goo. Many a discussion of cooking etiquette has ended with everyone diving out of the way of a flaming ball of goo that in its former life had been a marshmallow on a stick. Heady stuff for the Mallow Gourmands.

It doesn't stop there either. Do you place the mallow on the graham cracker first or does the chocolate go first? Do you toast the cracker and then place the mallow flambeau between two chunks of chocolate and then two Graham crackers? The pressure and etiquette is immense.

Personally, I recommend just chucking the whole thing. Leave the Marshmallows and Graham crackers at home. Why risk the social implications of serving dessert the wrong way?

Camp Coffee

If you can drink it without grimacing, it isn't camp coffee. I've tasted camp coffee so strong that the spoon to stir it with corroded away right before our eyes. You've heard of carbo loading? Experienced campers rely on Caffeine loading to get them through the day. How does one make this delicious nectar? (believe me, sometimes it pours so thick one might think it is nectar). Easy. Bring a pot of water to a rolling boil. Remove the pot from the fire, remember not to grab it with your bare hands. In theory, you add one teaspoon of coffee for every cup of water, but whose counting here? Grab a handful and toss it in. Doesn't look like enough? Grab another handful of grounds and add them to the slurry. Cover and let steep for five minutes or so, keeping the pot warm, but don't let the water reboil, otherwise you end up with coffee extract—not much different from regular camp coffee except that it is thicker. To settle the grounds add a drop or two of cold water and tap the side of the pot with a spoon. Now, decant off the coffee.

Take the first sip. Once your eyes realign you should be sure to thank the cook. Don't be alarmed by the somewhat gritty taste of the coffee. The grit is due to the few unsettled grounds that help to add

that special flavor and texture which is what makes camp coffee so memorable.

Doing Nothing is an Oxymoron

Every year, millions of campers head to the great outdoors to do nothing. Doing nothing is the great oxymoron and begs the question, how the hell can you do something if what you are trying to do is nothing which can't be done in the first place! Ahhhh the great mystery of life. At any rate, doing nothing on a camping trip is not possible. Why? Because no matter how hard you try to do it, something keeps coming up and getting in the way.

Turning the Other Cheek to the Wind

Camouflaged toilet paper (yes, there is such a thing, but why I have no idea) and inflate-a-potties (what happens if it happens to spring a leak when . . .well, never mind) are the trappings of a civilized society gone mad with trying to bring the conveniences of home to the wilds—what a ridiculous thought.

Still, there is much to be said for the perfect toilet spot, complete with a comfortable seat of rocks or a log and overlooking a great expanse of mountainous grandeur spreading beneath ones feet, or posterior in this case. I do caution everyone, as I have learned from personal experience and will share with a certain amount of trepidation, to take special care while perched at the edge of a steep slope. The thrill of an alpine view crap can only be overshadowed by one thing, watching the group's only roll of toilet paper bounce and tumble its way to the valley below—leaving a very visible trail of TP in its wake as it unravels its entire 500 foot length.

There are, of course, other dangers in hanging it all out in the wind and the wilds. Mosquitoes have a tremendous affinity, it seems, for anyone who will turn the other cheek. Balancing on a log with posterior on one side and feet on the other is dicey enough. The added excitement of swatting and swearing while doing one's business can be all too much for many folk. One friend, who, because I am a kind soul (and because he paid me an amazing amount of money to keep his name out of this text) went to swat an annoying mosquito on his hind quarters and ended up with a handful of . . .well, you get the picture. He was not a happy camper!

A few hardy souls are advocates of squat and deliver. This is a fine and dandy method if you can manage to keep your pants and underwear out of the target delivery zone (which many unfortunates do not) and if you have an outstanding sense of balance. If, however, you are like most folk, squatting with one's hind end hanging far enough out so as to miss the pants results in a disconcerting transfer of one's equilibrium. Once gravity has hold of the posterior, curling the toes and waving the hands desperately in the air is quite futile. In such a situation, I am afraid there is nothing to do but sit, bringing new meaning to the phrase "boy, you've gone and sat in it now!"

Campfire Myths and Lore

It took me awhile — almost three years of Boy Scouts and two years of summer camp — but eventually I learned that flexing your arm muscles while a mosquito is biting you will not cause the mosquito to explode. No doubt the few who sought to repeatedly convince me otherwise found tremendous hilarity in my "poor technique."

"Jeeze Mike," my best friend would say with mock concern, "you must not be doing it right, try it again only this time, really flex your arm muscle tight. I just can't believe you haven't popped one yet..."

Sure Rick. Why it never seemed a little suspicious that I was flexing while they were slapping is beyond me. Three hundred odd mosquito bites later, I learned that it is far better to swat and smile than lie in wait for the satisfaction of magically exploding an insect on my arm.

Every year, since the beginning of time, outdoor myths have been propagated by seemingly sage and compassionate outdoorsmen and women—often called as counselors, guides and close friends. These seemingly innocent myths are apt to cause physical and emotional damage to the numerous youths and adults who fall victim to them.

Perhaps you have heard or even experienced some of them. If you are a kind soul, then share the truth with your children and friends. Then again, maybe they should suffer like the rest of us. A few of the more common myths are:

- "You can keep all manner of wild animals away from your camp by carefully urinating around its boundary. Be especially careful

to soak the area around your food cache and tent." While this may have worked for Mowat in the movie "Never Cry Wolf," and has been tried for centuries by woodsmen to ward off wolves, it really isn't practical. It will, however, ward off all manner of friends who may have thought about camping with you and is sure to attract an amazing amount of interest if tried in a park campground.

- "Smoke always follows the most handsome or beautiful camper around the fire." This is just the kind of advice any choking and teary-eyed camper is looking for and is sure to make the recipient feel so much better — providing there is a tank of oxygen nearby after they pass out. Smoke is actually attracted to a vacuum of sorts, usually created by the tallest or largest object nearest the fire. If you are standing and the rest of the group is sitting, you will usually receive the smoke. If you build a small wall behind one part of the fire ring, and then all sit beside the fire on the opposite side of the wall, the smoke will rise in the wall's direction and not your eyes—does that mean it's a beautiful wall?

- "You know, if you place a small pebble in your mouth, you won't need as much water because the stone will draw water into your mouth." Brilliant! And just where is the water coming from? Your body of course. The author of this paragon of wilderness advice should be force to lick Half Dome from top to bottom. Two quarts of fluid per day per person, minimum. After that, you can suck on all the rocks you want.

- "Male fish are able to detect human female scent on a lure, and so they become more aroused into striking." A buddy of mine, Tom Stienstra, shared this gem with me recently after his wife had caught more fish than he for the third or fourth fishing trip in a row. I don't know if there is any truth to it, but then again, if my wife ever catches more fish than me I'll know the reason why.

6 Mosquitoes Are An Emergency, A Broken Nail Ain't

Bloodsucking Little Nasties

These denizens of the night, afternoon, evening, or anytime you are trying to enjoy yourself, thrive on taunting you. They buzz gaily around the inner space of your ear before probing for blood on any exposed portion of your bare anatomy. These little nasties are commonly called mosquitoes, otherwise known in scientific circles as *Bloodsuckus Disgustus*.

If one is a believer in evolution, you would have to suspect that mosquitoes evolved from the deepest, darkest forgotten piece of slime somewhere in the jungle—or New York City. If you believe in God and creation, then it stands to reason that mosquitoes were created to ruin otherwise perfect wilderness vacations and encourage us to return to the safety of a five day work week which no longer looks as bad as it did several days ago.

I have devoted years of haphazard and often frantic study to the research and methods of these blood sucking monsters. In

several parts of the globe, I am now cheerfully recognized and announced as the night's main course and entertainment. I have watched mosquitoes fight over who gets to jab me first and have learned over the years that, no matter how low the reported mosquito population is, I still manage to draw a capacity crowd. Because of my popularity, I have been able to study the mosquito as very few have, and wish to pass on what I have learned so that you can have a chance to enjoy your next vacation without worrying about this incessant scourge.

Glacial Streams Won't Stop Mosquitoes

I once heard that mosquitoes are heat sensitive and that people with lower temperatures are less susceptible to getting bothered. On one occasion, I immersed myself in a glacial runoff stream in an effort to lower my body temperature so that the mosquitoes would start enjoying my partners as much as me. The two second immersion lowered my temperature to such a degree that my body involuntarily began sprinting around camp waving its arms in an effort to get warm. The appearance of a blue and wildly frantic naked person caused my partners to believe I was being chased by something, so they bravely dove into the tent leaving the mosquitoes no choice but to eat cold cuts—which, by the number of bites I received were viewed as

48

quite a delicacy. First word of advice—stay out of glacial streams and be sure that your camping partners will stand and fight.

They Grow 'Em Bigger Up North

I once went backpacking with an old timer up in the Canadian Wilderness. Up there the air is so pure and the land so devoid of civilization you really feel as if you have escaped to a pine laden paradise. This should have been my first warning. Anytime you allow yourself to feel that you have stepped into paradise, your brain sends out an echo location signal drawing mosquitoes from as far away as Siberia. My second warning should have been the lack of other people. With few humans in the area, the mosquitoes are bigger, meaner, and far more desperate in their search for raw meat.

Did I mention bigger? Why one mosquito had a wing span of four feet and would have carried me away if the old timer hadn't hauled me into the tent—really, I'm not kidding! The old timer's theory as to not getting bitten was to ignore the little critters and make them think you don't care—this will hurt their feelings and they won't pay any more attention to you. I never had an opportunity to really test this theory. I was too busy running madly around camp slapping, cursing, tripping and generally providing entertainment for anyone who happened by. I found out later that the old timer made $30 selling seats to passersby who thought I was a traveling dance act.

Mosquito Repellent

Mosquito repellent is touted as a must in most circles. It seems that the manufacturers of this noxious substance have determined that the only way to repel mosquitoes is to liberally spread toxic waste on your skin, thereby shocking the little critters into flight or absolute submission. This seems reasonable as long as you can overlook the fact that all the plastic parts in your car, camera, and fishing gear are melting because you inadvertently spilled a drop or two when packing. Depending on

49

the species, I have found that mosquito repellent actually does one of three things:

1. Acts as a basting liquid preparing the skin to a moist but delectable texture and flavor that is viewed as a delicacy by most Canadian and High Sierra mosquitoes.
2. Causes mosquitoes to laugh hysterically as your skin slides off your hands, neck, and face. The one positive note is that while they are laughing they have a hard time biting.
3. Confuses the mosquitoes and redirects them to buzz around your head and inside your ears in a bewildered fashion, causing you to pound your skull repeatedly with your hand or a nearby skillet. This is perhaps the most dangerous side effect of repellent and has been known to cause ringing in the ears, large lumps, broken cooking implements, and sprained arms from all the wild swinging.

What should a camper do to protect against mosquito attacks? I have the answer. Never, ever give the impression that you are enjoying yourself, no matter how spectacular the scenery, good the fishing, or special the company. I was able to test this theory successfully one summer when backpacking with my wife—camping with a spouse is a widely accepted technique used to be sure one won't enjoy oneself.

We headed off on a three day journey to a remote lake (remote being defined as visited by less than 1000 people weekly), high in the Sierra Nevada. Soon we were groaning under the strain of carrying 700 lb packs and invoking the "I can't believe we are doing this for fun—this must have been your idea," clause. Things didn't get much better after we left the parking lot. The first night's camp in the valley, we ate cold gruel and huddled around a miserable sputtering stove. Several mosquitoes flew by, but seemed satisfied that we looked wretched enough so they continued on their way.

The following day our packs had somehow gained weight. Struggling with 1000 lbs. up a near vertical incline we broke through the clouds and into a glorious basin. Soft and fluffy, the clouds swirled below as we basked beside a blue jewel of a lake nestled among the mountain peaks whose sharp crags were etched against an azure sky. Already, we were using too many adjectives and our sentences were beginning to run on ridiculously. This was paradise. We should have known then we were doomed.

We struggled with the tent as the first wave of bloodsucking little nasties buzzed us. "I thought mosquitoes didn't live above 11,000 feet!", my wife yelled. "We must be having a good time or they wouldn't be here," I screamed above the roar. Amid the drone of incoming formations we ran for it.

Our wild, screaming, descent down the mountain cut a swathe through to the valley they are now using as a downhill ski resort. Hundreds of campers and several rangers joined in what became a mass exodus pointing desperately at, "a horrible apparition tumbling down the valley after us all." Calling that breathless and sweaty jumble of broken tent poles, torn fabric, mud, and various tree limbs a "horrible apparition," was an insult to my wife and next time I just won't stand for it.

Snuffle Snuffle Slurp

To the seasoned outdoorsman, there is nothing quite so chilling as hearing snuffle snuffle slurp just as pleasant dreams are about to chase the soreness of a day's hiking away. Snuffle snuffle slurp can mean one of two things. Either your camping partner has developed a case of sniffles while trying to gorge secretly on your highly prized personal stash of sweets, or Ursus americanus is rototilling his way through your pack in search of anything remotely edible.

When I was younger, several friends and I embarked on a teenage rite of passage in the Great Smoky Mountains. We were proud young men yearning for adventure and staggering under packs that quite possibly weighed more than we did. Our goals for the week were simple: develop finely honed mountain muscles to impress the girls; get completely dirty while having an amazing amount of fun; and make it back without getting eaten by bears. Personally, the last bit was thrown in because of our mothers who were fond of saying with a smile, "If you don't die of starvation first, the bears will get you for sure." That's what is great about mothers, they are always able to find just the right thing to say to put a young adventurer's mind at ease. Little did we realize then, but we were truly "Mere Mortals In Training."

Due to careful planning, starvation was not to be an issue. We had milk, eggs, bacon, bread, peanut butter, jelly, crackers, fruit, Koolaid, cereal, pudding, and a 50 pound stash of assorted candy bars. In fact, we had to leave our extra clothes behind just to make room for the emergency candy we might need if the trip went longer than expected. Bears however, were an uncertainty we knew we would have to face when the time arose. Although we had read that anything but the most casual of encounters was extremely rare, an uncomfortable, sort of tingly feeling lurked in the back of each of our young minds.

We were dropped off at the trailhead by our ever loving and considerate parents who offered this compassionate and sage advice, "Brush your teeth every day and don't let the bears get you." Thanks mom!

An old-timer, dressed in torn baggie jeans and a lumberjack-plaid shirt was sitting at the trailhead, grinning. "Ya'll watch out fer them bars now. If'n ya hears a sound like 'snuffle snuffle slurp', git yerself outa thar. That's the sound of a bar lookin for a snack an' he don't much care what the snack looks like. Have a safe trip now boys." Gee, thanks mister.

Our first night was at a lean-to structure made of logs with chain-link fencing in front to keep the humans in and the bears out. Kind of a reverse zoo situation. While we do the cooking, the bears and other animals get to look in and analyze humankind—hungrily. The drawback to this setup was the

restroom location. The engineer in charge must have forgotten that most people need to use the bathroom at night. Either that or he found it highly humorous to erect the outhouse 100 yards away from the protection of the chain link fence and down a narrow and very dark trail—did I mention dark?

Bathed in pre-dawn moonlight, the trail turned into a labyrinth of terror—I don't think one of us made it to the outhouse that night. Little wet puddles just outside the fencing evidenced quick decision-making on our parts. As it turned out, there was no outhouse anyway. Apparently, some idiot had dumped a six pack into the hole and a bear, unfamiliar with etiquette and doors, splintered the entire structure and left bits of Bud can and wood scattered everywhere. Great, now we had bears with a penchant for beer to avoid.

With our camp securely set-up for the second night, an amoebic looking clump of teenage bravado slunk and stumbled through the forest in search of firewood, ever on the lookout for drunken bears. With our arms loaded down and our nerves on edge, we returned gratefully to camp.

"Shhh! What's that?" hissed Dave.

"Cut it out you moron," returned Tad.

"No, really! There is something in our camp and it looks like a bear."

Our cluster of trembling humanity seemingly bonded and quivered apprehensively, pausing to breathe only when necessary. The huge hulking shape moved rhythmically with the wind.

"Jeeze, he's so drunk he can hardly stand up," I ventured. "Big too."

After about an hour of quivering and with the bear making no apparent move to leave our camp (except swaying every time the wind blew), we realized we had to do something. "Look," I whispered, "I read once that you should throw things at a bear to get it to move, you know, to chase it away."

Cautiously, and then with increasing abandon, we began chucking sticks, rocks, large branches, and handfuls of leaves. After five minutes or so of ground clearing fury, and after we ran out of all available ammunition, Dave whispered, "He's gone."

We cautiously crept back into camp. Sure enough, the bear was nowhere to be seen. All that remained was a mangled tent, buried under a pile of rocks, sticks, branches, and clumps of dirt.

"We killed our tent . . .you don't suppose. Look, we can't tell anyone about this, right?" We all nodded vigorously. "Man, that bear sure was huge huh?" I remember feeling distinctly grateful I had insisted on using Dave's tent and not mine.

Under a moonlit sky, and with Dave and Tad snoring the night away, I realized all the evening's activity had left me rather hungry. Carefully, not wanting to wake my friends, I popped the top off a can of Jello pudding. Unable to find my spoon, I resorted to licking "Snuffle, slurp, snuffle, slurp." Tad sat bolt upright in his bag and screamed, "Bear."

I leapt up, my sleeping bag draped around me. Dave and Tad screeched and pointed in my direction and began bounding, still in their bags, in the other. Realizing the bear must be right on my heels, I dropped the pudding and raced after them.

Fortunately, their trail was easy to follow. Bits of torn sleeping bag and large clumps of down leave a trail even a tenderfoot could follow. The large swath of broken trees and limbs, sheered off by two teenagers in the midst of a major panic attack, made traveling easy.

After a short while and upon catching up with my friends, I glanced behind me. Not noticing anything I slowed to a sprint, then to a jog, and finally to a brisk walk. "Hey, you guys," I panted, "he's not following us. Good thing I dropped that pudding I was eating, huh?"

Tad and Dave gave me a rather peculiar look. "Let's get him." It was a good thing I wore my tennis shoes—they might have really hurt themselves if they had actually caught me.

During the entire week, I don't think we ever really saw one bear. Sure, a lot of logs, in the twilight of life reared up and played serious havoc with our bladders and minds. We even had several large stumps and one giant boulder attempt to chase us down and maul us to death. However, through it all we learned to hang our food well away from camp, never take food to bed with us, make noise when traveling down a trail, never listen to grinning old-timers and parents when it comes to bear behavior, and always wear running shoes to bed—you never know when a good panic will require a need for speed.

Weather Happens

It doesn't matter what the weather forecast is, a camping trip is a sure fire way to encourage rain. Why state's in need of water don't voluntarily encourage the entire population to go on a weekend campout, thereby ensuring a statewide deluge of biblical proportions, I have no idea. It is also generally acknowledged that if it isn't raining anywhere else, it will always rain on or around a pitched tent.

First Aid Kit

A first aid kit is full of all sorts of goodies for solving minor medical emergencies—which to me seems to be somewhat of an oxymoron. If it is an emergency, how in the hell can it be minor. Mommy!

First Aid

If you are to believe most examples of first aid, as demonstrated so accurately by Hollywood, applying a tourniquet is the best remedy for any emergency.

Amid lots of dust and falling debris settling around the set.

"Sorry John, guess I shouldn't have pulled that root out huh."

"Owwww, I think you broke my arm you dweeb."

"Not to worry John, we'll just put a tourniquet around your neck and before long you won't feel any pain...John...hey,

John, where ya goin'?"

Of course, everyone knows that applying a tourniquet is only a last resort. First, you must determine if the victim has any medical insurance. Short of that, find out what his credit card limit is. Remember to always speak calmly to the victim.

"Relax Jerry, I once took a first aid class and I sort of remember what to do," you say in a calm, soothing voice.

"But Francis, it's only a blister, no big deal!" says victim, clearly panicked.

"Not to worry Jerry, that's what everyone says, but it's probably not as bad as it looks...here let me drain it," you calmly say as you begin heating your 8" knife blade over a flame.

"Really, Francis, just give me some moleskin and . . ." panic is increasing.

"Relax, I know what I am doing. I'll just cut here and...ooooo, I don't think it is supposed to bleed like that...not to worry, I'll just put on this handy tourniquet."

Notice how calm the rescuer remained in the face of rising panic. If it hadn't been for the composed and quick response of the rescuer the victim may have bled to death from the knife wound. The final step in this instance would be to leave the scene very quickly and cover your tracks.

Gee, It's Really Dark Out Here

With the increasing urbanization of our society, dark is becoming, well, darker. Looking from the inside of a house to the outside, darkness seems separate from existence, a kind of distant void that can be banished whenever by the simple flip of a switch. In the outdoors, however, darkness takes on an entirely different reality. It is for this reason alone that campfires were invented. The snapping and flickering flames provide a welcome barrier and security blanket of sorts against the myriad of rustles, snorts and grunts of darkness. Of course, these rustles, snorts, and grunts are probably just some poor camper fumbling with a

zipper in a desperate attempt to relieve himself, but then again, who's to tell.

Many visitors to the woods are equally surprised to find that it is at night, under the cover of darkness, when most things in the wilderness are active, not the least of which is the imagination.

Learning to recognize outdoor sounds

Yearggrewolmpphhh!: This is the sound a nocturnal wanderer makes as he trips over a tent guy line while making a nocturnal pilgrimage to the most holy of places, the latrine. It is also the sound emitted by a camper upon realizing that he has just stepped on his loose boot lace and that the only thing between him and the ground rushing up to meet him is his face.

OOOOOOohhhhahhhhhhheeeeeaahhh: This is the sound of a warm body sliding into a cold sleeping bag that has taken on all the comforting characteristics of an ice cube.

Yunnkahhhgrumphmmmm—oh god.: This is the sound of a person who, after having properly consumed one gallon of water during the day to prevent dehydration is now forced to come to grips with the fact that the sleeping bag zipper has jammed leaving him trapped to face a fate no one deserves.

John? Is that you . . .?: This is the sound of a camper who, while sleeping under the stars awaken to the feel of warm breath and the sound of sniffing in his ear.

Aieeeeeeeeeyeowowowowowow...: This is the sound from that same camper who is now sprinting madly up the nearest tree after realizing that John does not have a furry face or a cold nose.

Children and Wildlife

If it crawls or slithers and you have children along on your camping excursion, it is a safe bet that it will somehow find its way into a pocket for later study or worse, into a sleeping bag for entertainment. It is important to note that the camper whose luck it is to be chosen as the recipient of a garter snake in the sleeping bag will froth at the mouth and leap around for several minutes after discovery of the present. Not to worry, this is normal behavior and does not mean the child has rabies. It does, however, mean that you can be assured of one thing—the victim is already hard a work plotting the slow death of whoever placed the snake in his bag. No one to my knowledge has ever determined how a garter snake feels about freckles and down, but you can be sure that it isn't printable here.

Blisters

The one constant of any outdoor adventure is the blister. Like ants, they always manage to appear at the wrong moment and in precisely the wrong place, such as your feet instead of your friends. There are some recommended techniques for avoiding blisters, not the least of which is staying home and hiding in the closet.

Hiking with boots that are properly broken in is perhaps the best method of prevention, although I have found that it is not so much that the boots get broken in as the feet finally give up protesting.

Perhaps the most popular remedy for blisters is moleskin. Adhesive on one side and fuzzy on the other, moleskin makes it possible for battered feet to keep on truckin'. Personally, however, I never have gotten used to the idea of gluing a tiny mole to my foot just to soothe a sore spot.

7 Nature Study And Photography Are Grounds For Divorce

We head into the outdoors to commune with nature, to discover a part of ourselves that we don't know is missing but heard it is, so we're out to find it whatever it might be though we probably won't know what it is if it leapt up and bit us which many things do in the outdoors.

The Camera

Cameras are good for one thing only, documenting every moment and memory of the trip—from the greasy hair to the tan that will wash off after the first shower. I have taken many pictures of my wife, many of which have mysteriously disappeared. She claims that they never turned out.

Despite the best efforts to "disappear" photographic evidence which may prove damaging to one's ego, embarrassing slides continues to be a leading cause of divorce in America, or at least the spare bedroom getting lots of use. I once went to a friend's slide show of a mountain climbing trip he took with his wife in Nepal. Right smack dab in the middle of it was a larger than life photo of his wife trying to enjoy what she had previously thought was a very private moment communing with nature. While we all thought that we had never seen a more magnificent picture of a woman peeing in front of a mountain, she didn't appreciate the humor. Brad was left to resort to the ultimate degradation—plead and grovel in front of his pals for mercy. Good thing the fold out couch was a comfy one because I am sure that's where Brad spent his next month.

Wildflower Identification

Learning to identify wildflowers is one of those wilderness skills many of us have yet to fathom. Other than giving a good reason to stop and get out the guidebook, and of course giving guidebook authors something to do like write guidebooks, wildflower identification is right up there with, say, rock classification. I must confess that I am quite adept at identifying dandelions and daisies and will even go out on a limb sometimes to identify lupine and some of those other darn yellow composites that look like dandelions but aren't. Still, I've yet to realize the apparent thrill of thumbing enthusiastically through pages of flower pictures trying to key out an as yet unnamed plant.

"Betty, what did you say the color was," states Bob with nervous apprehension.

"Gee Bob, looks yellow to me . . .," comments Betty trying to sound interested.

"What kind of yellow Betty," queries Bob brimming with the thrill of the chase.

"Gosh Bob, kind of yellow like butter I guess, or maybe egg yolk . . .no the sun or maybe like a canary," states Betty struggling to stay focused.

"Damn it Betty, this is serious!. What kind of yellow?" stresses Bob, barely able to contain his apparent frustration at Betty's carelessness.

"Shoot Bob, I guess like a canary."

"OK, OK, OK, now are the leaves alternate, opposite or whorled . . .wait, no they're alternate, I can see that, so how high . . .hurry, measure it," says Bob, his voice rising in excitement.

"Oh Bob, I don't know, I guess two feet, maybe?" comments Betty, now clearly ready to move on.

"Two feet, alternate leaves and, oh my, canary yellow, oh, oh Betty oh my it's, it's a Dalmatian Toadflax . . .oh Betty, thank you, I'm drained."

"Gee, me too Bob . . .do you think we can go on now?"

"Give me a minute Betty, my knees are weak."

Artful Bluffing

There is a certain pleasure to be found in positively identifying something when you have absolutely no idea what it could be or even should be. If you are a parent, you know of whence I speak. How is it possible to deny an answer of great importance to the youth of the world, looking to you for guidance and the name of the flower at your feet?

"That," you should say, while assuming a distant and all-knowing stare and carefully stroking your chin "is a yellow-breath duckwort. Very rare in these parts."

The youth, ever in awe of your knowledge of the world will never be the wiser until he is older at which point hormones will override and erase all long-term memory cells and the incident will be forgotten.

Observing Wildlife

One of the main reasons many of us head out into the great beyond is to observe wildlife without bars between us and them and there is no better way to observe wildlife than through a camera lens.

Wildlife photography requires a special nerve, raw talent, and ability to overlook the obvious, like the fact that the bear is only inches away from the lens and apparently wants to discuss photo opportunities after lunch.

There are very few true outdoorspeople that wouldn't give just about anything to be able to bring home photos of wild bear tossing salmon in the air like so much sushi, or a mountain lion

slinking through the shadows after wild game. It is that dream
many would-be National Geographic photographers cling to as
they lug 15 pounds of camera gear along on every trip. It is also
that dream that drives people to attempt ridiculous feats of
bravado. "I had to climb forty feet straight up a cliff and hang by
one hand to get that shot of the brown hooded mountain hawk"
Those of us who are forced to sit through 900 identical shots of
this hawk can only roll our eyes and wonder why.

We are wondering why not because we are looking at 900
identical shots of a hawk, because if we could recognized a hawk
in any of the shots that would be truly special. We are wondering
why because every shot that is not blurred or overexposed is a
rear end shot.

That, my friends, is the essence of wildlife photography—
rear ends. I have an entire wall full of them. Deer butts, moose
butts, bear butts, eagle butts, even my wife's butt. Why do you
think they call them white tail deer or black tail deer? Because all
you will ever see of them is their butt.

Throughout eternity, the drill has always been the same.
One person points out the animal excitedly, "Wow, look, over
there!"

Immediately, the rest of the group begins searching wildly for a glimpse of whatever it is that looks like a Wow."

Of course, the person who spots the animal never has a camera. "John, quick, bring your camera and get a shot of this will you?"

John races forward, his fingers nervously thumbing the shutter release. Smoothly, he lifts the camera and looks toward the spot where the animal has been spotted and takes a picture of, yep, its butt.

If, by some miracle of miracles, the animal does not move off and offer up its backside for photographic posterity, one can be assured that the resulting picture will feature a speck in the middle of a great expanse of grass that the photographer will claim is the rare wild brown bear he spotted. All the magnification in the world will only make the spot look more and more like a spot. Still, it's a spot that the would-be Galen Rowell is very proud of.

Foraging

Many campers thrill to the idea of supplementing their basic cold and freeze-dried diet with fresh food. The concept of self-sufficiency is indeed an admirable one, but that is why supermarkets were invented, because everyone knows that if we had to spend time foraging for food, we wouldn't have time for the really important things in life like TV and frisbee.

While, in theory, foraging offers the prospect of fresh greens and perhaps fish to supplement the backcountry diet, what happens in reality is an entirely different story.

"Found these leaves that the guidebook says are edible."

"Great, let's sprinkle on some dressing and then ACCCKKKKK!"

"Petuieeee, these taste terrible."

"Pass me the Snickers and Cheez-Its."

Thus endeth yet another noble attempt at foraging.

8 The Summer Camp Training Program—Learning To Pee In Cursive

No book about the outdoor experience would be complete without a section on summer camps. Thousands of us "merely mortal" experts gained our wealth of knowledge and backcountry experience while at camp, whether it was with the Scouts, YMCA, private camp, or another organization.

Why parent's send their kids to camp

We have summer camps because if we didn't parents and children would be forced to spend an entire summer together getting

on each other's nerves. For parents, camp is an opportunity for peace and the chance to rediscover that romance and a clean house were things that were too often taken for granted in 10 BC (Before Children). For children, it is a marvelous opportunity to discover the meaning of freedom and a litany of important outdoor skills such as sustained burping and belching in song.

Freedom at camp, however, is a relative term and can be best understood by looking at the four types of freedom available (one will observe that this is nothing more than the age-old survival of the fittest):

1. You are an older camper thereby establishing yourself as a leader of people, boys, mice, whatever. As an older camper it becomes your responsibility to show the younger campers how to communicate colorfully and in a way that leaves those of us classified as adults baffled as what was just said; how to write home during letter writing time to someone else's mother about the rattlesnakes and rabid bear terrorizing camp and not get caught; how to sneak off to the girl's camp after lights out and make it back alive after being chased by a rabid bear that usually turns out to be the girl's camp head counselor. As you can tell older campers must shoulder a tremendous responsibility regarding care and upbringing of younger campers.

2. You have a brother who is an older camper. If this is the case you can usually get yourself out of most trouble with other campers or into more trouble with counselors by casually revealing during tense moments, "My brother is . . ."

3. You are bigger than the other kid's older brother and all the other kids in the cabin. This provides an important outlook on freedom— freedom to choose your bunk, your locker, your slaves.

4. You are smarter than the bigger kid and make lots of friends, one of whom happens to be the counselor in charge of your cabin.

As I was a very small camper, I found great value in option #4, and quickly set about calculating how to make a massive amount of friends in a short time—one of these being the counselor of course. To begin on my friendship quest I first had to avoid being made a slave by the huge kid with big ears, no neck, short hair, wearing an army jacket who was walking my way. As it turned out I needn't have worried—he was the counselor. I just wish I would have known this before locking myself in my trunk.

Acquiring Outdoor Skills

I didn't realize it at the time, but the summer of 1968 was, for me, a major step toward becoming an experienced camper and a man. Granted, in later years I kept slipping off the step, but, because of that summer, I at least knew how to climb back on.

Camp serves a very important purpose in the grand wilderness scheme. Without camps, kids would have a much harder time acquiring vital woods skills such as peeing in cursive, learning to identify the difference between a raisin and a dead fly (especially useful if Raisin Bran is on the menu), boiling an egg in a paper cup, burning the hairs of the back of your friend's hand with a magnifying glass, and lighting a match with your zipper or your teeth (dentists love that one.)

Two other very important skills also get honed at camp. On demand farting, something every parent becomes so proud of their children for when summer camp is over, and mumblty peg. Mumblty peg is an idiotic game whose sole purpose is to provide a reason for the camp to have a nurse. The game involves very sharp knives, fingers and sticking the knife in a surface as close to fingers as possible without touching them. There is a theory that this one game alone is responsible for some men (you never see women playing this) losing touch with their senses and getting the bright idea that for camping to be fun it must involve weaponry and large knives—the more the better.

Bottom Bunks Are For Dweebs

Top bunks are coveted for many reasons and a top bunk near the door—well that is the ultimate. It is important to realize that every day becomes a test of mastery in the survival regimen of a camper and knowing what bunk to select is just another valuable skill. These same territorial skills are critical in later years as one learns to seek the best campsite, the one sleeping space near the door of the tent, the last Hershey bar.

It is at camp, however, where these important life survival skills become honed. You never know for instance whether someone, usually a thoughtful older camper trying to provide an educational experience for younger campers, might remove the springs supporting the upper bunk mattress. Properly executed, this removal results in the upper mattress becoming the lower usually sometime after lights out. If you are lucky enough to be in the upper bunk you experience the thrill of freefall. The one in the lower bunk begins to understand the meaning of "flat as a pancake."

It is also common knowledge that those in the bottom bunk are completely subject to the whims of the upper bunkee. The camper climbing into the upper bunk is required by some indefinable force to find a secure foothold for each upward and downward journey on a cheek, stomach, or other area we won't mention of the unfortunate groveling on the lower mattress.

Perhaps the worst fear of any camper relegated to a bottom bunk, worse than being buried under two-ton Charlie's freefall, worse than being stepped on by feet that smell as if they've been embalmed in leather boots since birth, is the fear of an uncontrolled bladder in the upper bunk.

Being near the door had the benefit of offering quick exits. Exits from a cabin become important during reveille when 300 bladders come to grips with the realization that there are only 15 toilets. Equally important is the need to execute a quick and unobstructed exit after one of the cook's special meals. An often overlooked need for a quick exit is after a particularly heinous prank has been played upon a larger camper and it is fairly obvious that you, the snickering small camper, has committed this foolish act and is now in danger of becoming an extinct camper. Any experienced camper will tell you that the only thing keeping you from the

infirmary in this situation is a skillful demonstration of raw speed and agility in executing an extremely difficult move consisting of dressing, opening the door, and disappearing for a week all within one fluid action. Increasing the difficulty of this move is the probability that the hands of one very upset larger camper will be attempting to remove your head from your body, stuff it in an envelop, and mail it home to your parents.

The Beast

I am not certain what comes over adults in a camp environment, but it does seem that it is the mission of every decent counselor to completely and utterly terrorize his/her cabin at least once during the course of a summer. I am not referring to harmless nature stories about bears or wolves here. It seems that whenever children and adults are placed together in a camp or outdoor setting the inevitable story of a one eyed, hairy, fanged, axe wielding, one armed, burned beyond recognition, headless, one legged, slimy, murderous creature of the swamp, lake, mountain, cabin or other location as seems appropriate to the mood and location, gets told.

Beasts usually get first sighted lurking in the shadows (all good beasts do a lot of lurking before serious carnage occurs). Following a week or so of lurking, the real terrorizing begins. One night after a council fire a camper who was lagging behind disappeared. His body is found half eaten the following day beside the dining hall. Next a camper is nabbed when going to the bathroom at night and his body is found half eaten (seems this guy can never get a full meal) at the archery range. Later in the week, two campers who apparently skipped the evening sing-a-long (I still am not sure which is worse, a sing-a-long or a dangerous beast) turn up mauled beyond recognition at the front gate.

This starts a giant beast-hunt (for a scary story to have credibility, you can never start a beast hunt until more than two or three campers have been killed). Of course the beast gets cornered and after a struggle, a struggle in which no counselor is even so much as scratched, the beast gets burned alive in a wood shed. Funny thing though—no bones, ax, or other evidence of the beast are ever retrieved from the ashes of the wood shed. And, several of the counselors, who of course were campers during this terror reign, now report seeing single foot prints around camp and strange ax marks in cabin doors in recent weeks.

It doesn't take much imagination to realize that to survive the remaining weeks at camp following the revealing of the hideous presence of the beast, campers must stick together. Like little models of amoeba, campers grope and glide around camp in groups of 3 or more (it is a known fact the beasts cannot harm you if you are in a group of three or more). Sing-a-longs get perfectly attended, no one dares lag behind after council fires, flashlights are carried in each hand, and serious retentive skills are developed and honed during many a night vigil for sunlight and blessed porcelain relief.

However, there were some serious flaws in camp monsters. For instance, what do they do when camp is not in session? And, if this beast is so dangerous, how is it that no counselor has ever been mauled? Furthermore, and I pointed this out to my counselor while I was a camper, how is it that only counselors have been sighting him because in our several hundred or so group forays to the girl's camp we hadn't seen or heard a thing—whoops.

Fortunately, my no neck counselor had a sense of humor. During the hour or so that I was left hanging from the rafters in my Jockeys it occurred to me that maybe I had seen this beast. Yeah, I mean that might not have been the girls' camp head counselor chasing us. Come to think of it we weren't so much being chased as hopped after. Either way, being caught by a beast or a raging, foaming-at-the-mouth girls' camp head counselor spells doom and despair—wait a minute, maybe the girls' camp head counselor was the beast.

9 Ask Calvin Camper: The Outdoor Survivalist's Guide To Wilderness Skills And Other Useless Information

Dear Calvin,
Q: Why is the first day of a hike always the hardest?
A: Due to the reduced air molecule concentration at the higher altitudes of the earth's atmosphere and because we are a "kinder and gentler nation" your body doesn't have sufficient time to acclimatize to the fact that you are seriously going to try and cram one week's worth of wilderness vacation into two days because you have to be back at work on Monday.

Dear Calvin,
Q: How much does a quart of water weigh?
A: What is this, a trick question? Everyone knows that a quart of water weighs two pounds until it gets placed in your pack at which point, through an unfathomable chemical process, it gains weight geometrically ending up with a weight of anywhere between 6 to 600 pounds.

Dear Calvin,
Q: What is a cairn?
A: A cairn is a man-made pile of rocks used to mark a route that crosses an open area where street signs and roads haven't yet been constructed.

Dear Calvin,
Q: My pack always seems to weigh too much. What can I do?
A: Leave the unabridged version of War and Peace, the Nintendo, and the Sony Surround Sound CD/TV at home and, while I empathize with your need for creature comforts, might I suggest that the Cappuccino maker is taking it a bit too far?

Dear Calvin,
Q: How can I tell if I am drinking enough fluids?
A: If your skin begins to take on the texture of dried paper and your mouth starts to taste and feel like the Sahara Desert you can be fairly sure that you need to drink fluids. One way to prevent this feeling is to drink copious amounts of water during the day which will leave you with an insuppressible urge to pee once you slide into your sleeping bag and zip the tent up.

Dear Calvin,
Q: What is bushwhacking?
A: Bushwhacking is a term used to denote cross-country travel without the benefit of a trail or nearby Howard Johnsons. It is so named because, after several hours of whacking bushes in search of a trail, your partner will begin to wonder aloud about your legendary wilderness skills and you will begin to feel an overwhelming desire to whack your partner with the nearest available bush.

Dear Calvin,
Q: I just got a compass and have been trying to figure out how to reverse direction once I have been following a bearing of 180 degrees for several miles.
A: Just turn around you idiot. Seriously, this is called reverse navigation and is a complex skill that involves using Pythagorean theory and geometric processes known only to

High School math teachers who enjoy watching their students squirm while trying to figure out problems someone else has already found the answer for making the entire process unnecessary in my opinion. I mean, if someone has already done it, they why do it again.

Dear Calvin,
Q: What part of the body is most susceptible to heat loss?
A: The head. A body loses up to 70% of its heat through the head. Of course, there are those breezy occasions, during the call of nature, when one would swear that the head is certainly not the part of the body most susceptible to heat loss, especially when an ice-cold hand is introduced to the equation.

Dear Calvin,
Q: Why is camping so popular?
A: Because every camper is affected with the same condition, short term memory loss. You can carry a 500 lb pack up and over Mt. Miserable with bleeding blisters on your feet, get rained on the entire time, eat nothing but burned slop and return home swearing that you will never again go camping. But you will. Because once you are at home and begin recounting the tale of your trip a strange thing begins to happen. It becomes harder and harder to remember what it was that you didn't like about the trip and all you can say is that you had a marvelous time and have never felt so free in all your life. After several days, you will actually begin sounding like Julie Andrews and may in fact spontaneously break into a stirring rendition of "The hills are alive . . ." Not to worry, this is all normal.

Questions Worth Pondering
'Cause Calvin Doesn't Have the Answer

Why is it that emergencies never happen when the sun is shining and the weather calls for Coppertone?

Why is it that the only time you get confined to a tent during a storm, your partner, who is never of the opposite sex, takes this opportunity to clean their nails or take up yodeling?

Why is it that the one item you need now is always at the bottom of the pack?

Why is it that the rope you brought to hang food with to keep it away from bears is always a few inches too short instead of a few inches too long?

Why is it that flashlights always work perfectly anytime but at night when you need them most?

Why is it that the only time your air mattress develops a leak is the one time when you forget to pack a patch kit?

Why can't someone invent dehydrated camping gear that you add water to once you arrive at camp? Sure would make carrying a tent a whole lot lighter.

Why is it that the only time your camping partner mentions a bad back or trick knee is when you are dividing the gear at the trailhead?

Why is it that no matter how you set up a tent, you are always the one sleeping with your head downhill?

Why do rainstorms always occur when your raingear is packed away in the deepest, darkest, and most inaccessible corner of your pack?

Why is it the rainstorms always stop several minutes after you have struggled to put on your raingear?
Why is it that no matter how big your backpack is you never seem to have enough room?

Why is it that tents are always built to accommodate one person less than the number actually going on the trip?

Why is it that the one spot you plan to visit is always located at the corner of four different maps?

Why is it that the one solitary leak in any tent is always on your side?

Why is it that the weight I lost on the last trip always manages to find me at home?

Why is it that a campfire always inspires the one's with the worst voice to break into song?

Why is it that any singing around the campfire usually involves Home on the Range, She'll Be Comin' Round the Mountain, Blowing in the Wind or 100 Bottles of Beer on the Wall?

Why doesn't the Forest Service require ranchers to clean up after their cows?

Why ask why?

Index

Mountain Biking for Mere Mortals
by Michael Hodgson

Mountain Biking for Mere Mortals
by Michael Hodgson
$6.99 paperback • $8.99 Canada
6x9 inches • 96 pages • 44 cartoons and
drawings • index • glossary
ISBN 0-934802-82-3

bumps and bruises. Glue yourself back together. Explore racing to destroy ego, body and bike while surrounded by friends. Also included is a mountain bike survivalist's dictionary of necessary and ridiculous terminology.

A humorous and unorthodox look at mountain biking through the eyes of a mere mortal. Too often, books on the subject of mountain biking focus on the efforts of lycra clad dare devils on bonsai missions. Well now the not-so-gonzo-but-still-totally-committed enthusiast will learn techniques for mountain biking by learning what is perfectly unacceptable.

This book ain't for "team scream" lycra clad bikers with huge thighs and lime green ultra-bright neon duo-tone bikes with the name "Wild Thing." It's simply for mere mortals.

About the author:
Michael Hodgson is an award winning outdoor journalist/author and a member of the Outdoor Writers Association of America. In addition to this book he has written *The Basic Essentials of Weather Forecasting* and *The Basic Essentials of Minimizing Impact on the Wilderness*. He currently resides in San Jose, CA where he writes an outdoor column for the San Jose Mercury News and is a contributing editor for Backpacker Magazine.

Discover riding techniques to help avoid near death and other such unpleasantries. Use etiquette which will not dismay hikers, equestrians and other bikers. Care for your steed and master maintenance skills that can be performed with a mallet. Tour from your back yard to the wilderness or go where no sane person would think of going. Prevent injuries,

LOOK FOR NEW *MERE MORTALS*
BACKPACKING, IN-LINE SKATING, SKIING
SURVIVAL, CANOEING, RAFTING